DESCENDANT

DESCENDANT
MARIANNE BORUCH

WESLEYAN UNIVERSITY PRESS
Middletown, Connecticut

For Will

Copyright © 1989 by Marianne Boruch

Thanks to the editors of the following journals for first printing these poems, some in versions now slightly revised: *The American Poetry Review, The Antioch Review, The Beloit Poetry Journal, College English, Denver Quarterly, Field, Graham House Review, The Iowa Review, The Kenyon Review, The Massachusetts Review, The Nation, The North American Review, Northwest Review, Prairie Schooner.*

"My Son and I Go See Horses" appeared in *The Pushcart Prize XIV* (1988-89).

All inquiries and permissions requests should be addressed to the Publisher, Wesleyan University Press, 110 Mt. Vernon Street, Middletown, Connecticut 06457

LIBRARY OF CONGRESS CATALOGING-IN-PUBLICATION DATA
Boruch, Marianne, 1950–
Descendant / Marianne Boruch. – 1st ed.
p. cm. – (Wesleyan poetry)
ISBN 0-8195-2160-4 ISBN 0-8195-1161-7 (pbk.)
I. Title. II. Series
PS3552.07564D4 1989
811'.54 – dc19   88–21117
CIP
Manufactured in the United States of America

This book is supported by a grant from the National Endowment for the Arts.

FIRST EDITION

WESLEYAN POETRY

Contents

III

I

My Son and I Go See Horses

Always shade in the cool dry barns
and flies in little hanging patches like glistening fruitcake.
One sad huge horse
follows us with her eye. She shakes
her great head, picks up one leg and puts it down
as if she suddenly dismissed the journey.

My son is in heaven, and these
the gods he wants to father
so they will save him. He demands I
lift him up. He strokes the old filly's long face
and sings something that goes like butter
rounding the hard skillet, like some doctor
who loves his patients more
than science. He believes the horse

will love him, not eventually,
right now. He peers into the enormous eye
and says solemnly, I know you. And the horse
will not startle nor look away,
this horse the color of thick velvet drapes
years and years of them behind the opera,
backdrop to ruin and treachery, all
innocence and its slow
doomed unwinding of rapture.

Raising Lumber

Houses in that weather rose up
like brand-new dice flung absently
after midnight. We turned the days
in crisp blue shorts. Irons awkward on their boards
hissed like insects, searing linen
behind the driveways, the half-grown trees.

My mother planted crab apple, small knobby things,
a luminous flowering in awful wet springs,
pink or white in daylight, after dark
no color at all but thin moody trembling
over the yard. My brother left us
for the basement, grinding his telescope mirror
like a mantra. Chemicals festered above the cracked
concrete. Everything slanted

toward the drain where a fishhook descended, "just
in case." *Just in case,* I repeated into
litany for weeks, as the wire
looped and grew dusty, and nothing
from the inner planet stirred. So stones

turned ancestor, or anyone
in sleep. Those afternoons I stood, an eye
in the needle, out toward the yard. Next door,
Frankie Corea continued pounding out a treehouse
from his father's shed, ripping up, then
raising lumber, as if some ancient tomb
were opened, and once opened, robbed
half with delight, half dread.

The Fox

Someone was kind and poisoned the fox,
a bright hour for setting out the flag
to warn, saying sweetly, here fox
here. O cloud,
inviting darkness
to the moon. I stopped the car
and wandered in that wood
an hour, to another life
a fox bloated
and no longer a fox
but a window in that room
years ago, where ashtrays
never emptied, where you smiled and shrugged,
where neither of us knew enough
to tell the truth. Sweet poison
in those years was sweet enough
to linger on and on.
We invited darkness
there. You said, clouds
cover the moon too much.
A man set a red flag against the tree
not a mile from that window.
We didn't know yet
what such flags mean. We said
how pretty against those leaves.

After Supper in Madison, Wisconsin

Where they come from, I do not know
these dead
walking off their old confusions, 1928
or 1941, the war
just beginning over Sunday dinner.
Here gables in high roost
over forsythia, the same drunken bluebells
slow the vibrant grass.

I am walking west, early May, toward the end
of the century. Silence.
The dead hear it, nothing
but birds
louder than cars. Like a small child
the street wanders: brick   wood   airy trees.
Whole families lost
in such houses where memory presses
its body back into doorways and rooms. *I've
    got to know,* the dead
hiss, rigid at the windows, correcting,
quarreling. Gradually
porchlights claim each landing anyway
calling *home   home.*
Darkness sets adrift the rest.

It's spring and spring and spring—as though
a mystery
to be found at the bottom of a sack.
So what, the dead whisper. So I look past
the new railing—the girl
in the day-glo sweatshirt
leaning icily against the slate blue door.
I am polite
to these dead, say, it *is* the same girl,
1928, 1941, the one you hated or loved
or just didn't believe. Cars
creep down the boulevard,
barely hum. And yes—the same boy, sullen,
lingers on the steps.

The Fat One in Her Lifetime

In that body, there are years when nothing's happened,
months curled limp against the drag
of heart and lung. Every cell's asleep. My great-aunt extracts

herself from the moaning Buick
as if against her will. My grandmother peers
behind the curtains. She adjusts the swan,
its raging ruby eye, below her collar. *O Aileen,* the famous
fat one said, *why so tasteless?* Stubbornly, it startles
the sad gray dress.

Good God, she's here. So this
is glee. In lemonade, in Fig Newtons piled
to near collapse, darkness gathers
its fevered points in glad cahoots. My aunt is almost
to the door. So my grandmother coins
her reserve of ice, swiftly now

above our grinning, as winter does, rerouting streets
in one fantastic November night. I am called
to kiss the fat one's firm mustache, to sit

absorbed. I count twenty roses fading up the wall
above her head. As usual, she brings
records thick as fingers, trespassed pale
with scratches: white men
playing black men who leer about a dog,
a saw, a branding iron. The Victrola

rattles. The fat one's laughter
swoops alone against the ceiling
like a rabid bird. My grandmother, as usual: *at least
she's not contagious.*

House Moving

80 feet, they said, to move the house
back 80 feet, a backyard
into a frontyard. So the thing's hoisted up
like some county fair stunt. We walked down
and watched, took every
dinner guest who,
as usual, dropped in.
The kids were bored—the adults, amazed
as children, they told each other.
It can't be so great
for the house, one said, the house suddenly
not a house but
a playhouse: little curtains
in the window, a rocker happy as a metronome.
It all rolled by.
Really, you said to me, if we
moved ours, we would see
the river from our bedroom window.
We could watch it freeze into a street
in winter. We could clock it
like a goblet to break
in spring under the shrill grinding
of the last daredevil pickup.
Everyone around us
had the same idea: move it all,
the whole world 80, 90 feet
and launch ourselves senselessly giddy
into a future already
laid like a table,
its tiny forks and knives trembling
only a little.

After the Hurricane

On a morning like this, every leaf is jubilant,
happy for its life, nodding to St. Jude,
mentor of dead ends, vigilante
against quicksand and ruts. I pull back
the curtains, and let all of it in: the maple
roused out of bad news, giving off its steady light.
Luck happens like an egg. We boarded up
the house, stacked, then covered winter's
wood, took every shaking toy into the dark garage
for peace. All night, the house swayed and mourned
like Buddhists at a mother's wake. Outside, some
radio spawned cheap, dismal rock, quirky
now and then, as if in flight. It seeped through walls.
You slept into another life right next to me. No one
to ask. And now this day, shrugging off the past
like so many other stupid accidents—of birth
or even love. Forget it, just go on, chants
the blinding, damaged air.

In Starlight

On other planets, light does not startle
but lies there certain
of the rocks it skims, as coolness knows everything
over water. So many places with Earth god names: Mars,
this Venus over your shoulder, then you
spin me around in starlight, pointing,
if it were visible, that's Jupiter. If
it were visible, I think, as roses
retreat in darkness
to nothing but shape, the trellis
a pale scaffold braced against the house.
House. I stare it
out of shadows—chairs around a table there,
apples half-witted in a bowl. My grandmother,
dead some sixteen years, is humming
nothing I remember, walking through the porch
cautiously, as if it were a rabid stretch of moon.
She stops to pick up something
darker than the air. *And there,* you nod,
that would be Saturn. How close
we are. I can barely
make you out. Your arm is raised
against the heavens. *If only it were
visible,* you say again.

1957

Passing through trees, I believe my friends
children again, driven
heat-mad, loading the car
with too much chicken, an old Coke cooler
whose glassy sides take light
and bury it in ice. Picnic: a word on the tongue
a cool mint
20, 30 years ago,
long before I met any of them,
before the terrible prosperity
that made us all in the 8th grade put down
the sacred fountain pen for its sleazy ballpoint brother.
The Chevy's hot, windows rolled down
hard against the hard hot wind.
Next to Susan and Peter, a boy
sits—I don't know him—jammed among them, he
watches a fly
go berserk with rage. Someone's mother
drives. Someone's mother
who's had it: every bickering minute
crowding out a life
that was too small to begin with. Chaos
in that car
moving down a summer day in 1957.
Voices that will quiet in so many years,
call lawyers, whisper love
and then deny it—now, shrill brats joyously roaring
their heads off
at every passing root beer stand. All but the boy
still watching the fly, completely, as though
religion were real, a glow in the head, a ticking silence.
What of him? Or of next week when he enters
my life, grown sardonic, still secret. And what use
are poems? I won't know him. I won't.

Flies

Spring, and the filth returns
in little mutinous packs.
My mother-in-law
insists, and brings us flowers
sullen in their ribboned paper, then
blinking wildly out of jars
we set for them like traps.
My son is three, and looks outside.
More spring, he says, pointing to the yard
no longer snow, but sodden,
beaten down like some awful
something leaked
in earth. I know there is
a god for this. We offer up
our restless rootless flowers.
But these flies
or whatever these tiny creatures are
know more about the inner life,
its worthless remedy of remorse,
its anguish
jubilant and incomplete.

A Deck of Cards Thrown to Wind

The treehouse was my heart
and the flung cards children tore and left
my levitation. It was neither wind
nor joy. It was more
my sorrow which held them high
and made them swim midair.
I watched them
from the porch, blank
with that little endless afternoon
which took years
to get through, childhood, and the backyard
rich in trees. But beyond, the stunted crab apple
violent, taking aim.

When I passed my neighbor's barn today
there was one bale
suspended, creaking only a little
as it swayed and burned
a shadow of itself on the slow cold floor.
It pinned my eye, and I stood

like a kid, released
into the cruelty of things.

Buick

On the rusting fender of the old
Buick, I lay down my head
and watch the field blur with flowers,
clouds in their noble boredom
drag the sky bluer as they

pass. But this is winter, and I'm inventing
what leads me out of my life,
a set of intricate pulleys, gift
of the boy genius in the basement—my brother
maybe—who begged off school to get on with things.

Nothing shakes this field: eventually
shadows sift into grass, earth
cools by evening, and not like music.
This Buick was my father's. I'm sure of that.
He drove it here drunk. He parked it here

gracelessly, and sat with years
bunched behind him, which is to say
he thought of nothing, squinting down
the glare. So my family figures things. We stop
until the fury dwindles down to ash, what

would be bone. Perhaps an archaeologist could
find us; one xeroxes an unreadable something
through winter's half-afternoon. I see
that narrow room, his face moon-desolate
and slack. As for the fitful shaft of light

pure as fishhook, it is grief
or something worse.

The Flood Plain

The flood plain began behind that house
without a trace of vengeance, just
summer growth, the lush everything green
stinging, singing
with small metallic life.
You could sleepwalk
to the river. I imagined how,
from a great height, we'd look
caught in shards of light, our journey
simple momentary color. Below the river stilled,
a slim jelly of glass
the bank as if grief were sown
years, the averted eye, suddenly
of strangers. You handed me the child.
His eyes were running dreams. Overhead
something dripped. Your shirt
blue, torn, the one
you loved: all I could see of you
passing through strange
haywire trees, the flood plain
bursting now, choking light.
I closed the child against me. He wanted night.
Sullen birds too high to see
warned, leaf warned
in silence. The river crept before us
biding, biding.

The Doctor Far from Home

At the auction, several men are dying of cancer.
Not six months, says my friend
as we stand in the back of the place
holding back our bids. An old man
suddenly rises, his face
alert and spectral as a sliver of moon.
He nods and smiles. My friend waves back happily
as if there were reason.

You could be wrong, I say
walking through the cold parking lot, past
the pickups and the beat-up Fords.
He shrugs, as though, yes, he could misplace
a scarf, even an expensive one.

At our house, his wife is saying: I can't go to him
for my problem. He can't bear to examine me.
We're drinking beer, waiting
for the roast, for potatoes to soften.
On the porch, my husband hoists
our son, spinning him wildly on the faded linoleum.
Through the window, we watch them.

Blur in the Attic

I look across roofs
summer, a fan spinning
its drugged eye into a gable
there: a bed, a landscape
on the wall—woods, all trees and wonder—then
a ledge where a birdnest
murmurs, moss-covered, still intact.

Nothing stirs, but the fan whirls
hot hot in that room, an anguish
so tight it is undisturbed for years, a thorny flame
within the heart, the way the young have
of putting their bodies
into the sad heat of things and staying there.

A boy and girl sleep on, or pretend
to sleep. Bed narrow as a board. That light
I know, falling of an afternoon.
This house is wood and brick and wood.
I'm old. Someone fills the attic nerve

where days I had once sagged and leapt,
cramped, as I read the required dose.
Wordsworth, Musil, Whitman, Yeats:
witness in that room again.
The girl hollows herself around the boy.
Everything begins by being dreamt.

Reasons

In the first place, the sky lit
always, with cheerful indifference.

You were on your way
to a crucial dignity, earned
by remembering everything.

I remember this much: a wooden boat, turned over
in grassy shade, midsummer.
Nearby, the water stirred and wandered.
I still hold it in my head.
My defense. My rescue.

Your pale body disappeared as you swam
to the other side. Glimpses of you
gleaming. Your steady rhythm

and the thought that if I shouted
you'd hear nothing. Enough
to be breathing, roar of blood
in the secret inner ear.

How I ran my days: to no purpose,
the refrain the refrain of crickets.

crickets

So I gave up the evening to them also.

In the second place
the boy came between us
like a happy glue. He copies

our restlessness, says
senseless solemn things.
I take him in my arms, say
tree, say
leaf, say
good night yard. So he
waves, unstoppable as cars that pass
night that crushes.

We are suddenly the memory
and future of ourselves, slipping through

the screendoor
saying, bed now, time for bed.

Third place: a continual slow surprise
at your beauty
which is a kind of country.
I take my citizenship seriously. I handle
my passport with care,
your name as ready on my tongue
as body warmth and taste
is there.

I tell you
the air was wonderful near the lake today
bringing back days
we knew better, but not
so much.

Table of celery onion tomato lettuce.
I mix the olive oil.
You cover the chicken with a kind of blessing
soy sauce, garlic.

The boy on the floor
rattles the clothespin against the open drawer.

In the kitchen silence, I hear cars
outside. I hear the world, innocent
of us, pass on.

Napping in Trees

Forget the orchard. Here
a field opens and the elm
is painfully obvious. I look up,
generations shimmering inhuman and perfect, the leaf
only partially conscious, its mute side
turned down to me, sleep
all its groceries gathered.

Here is food we call light.
Or patience we call it, forbearing summer.
Or tedious, on glaring afternoons.

But I have walked out to trade
into a quiet shade, and light
is changing into something: citizens of oxygen
slipping brilliant into air.
I follow them into their country. I want
to be so faithful, how the bird
travels full way, autumn rot
pressing downward into spring anyway,
in spite of. I begin

to climb. There is always wind. Behind that
these pleasant lies as though
driving all night even the children
go pale and dreamy
straight into folktale, simplified
by dark. As it always is. The world
is flat. Believe though.

Trees are breathing.

II

Perennial Garden

In the garden, I followed your eye,
called them lamb's ear and primrose,
stroked the small alert faces
turned up like sparks of a distant moon.
And forgot this was an afternoon in May,
forgot I was a woman and a mother.
How high we were, the houses below specks
of angular darkness. You moved
in and out of shade, suddenly far away soothing
the fierce new flowerheads, their
busy electric yellow. Then the moment
passed, and I was human again. Over and over
I asked you names, hungry
for something, as if we could coin color
and substance and scent
right there, out of black earth.
The owner let us roam—strangers—she, trusting
of a certain wonder. Look, you whispered,
look at these lilies of the valley. . . .
In a perfect hush we stood
world so conscious and all at once
all of it indifferent to us
as if we had no names, as if our lives, edged
and thick and dragged for years behind us,
had never happened.

White Rose

Once this rose knew too much.
Our grandmothers moved easily among its small rooms
and radiant furniture, our grandmothers
as stubborn girls again, hoarding us inside them
in clusters, grape by grape, saying things
like: not me. I'll never be a mother.

Of course no one believes such truth.
The rose is a liar anyway, its fabulous perfume
proof—though even the mailman, his eyes
like tiny hardened cranberries, slows past its ornate
staged longing for a moment
sweetened, like a glass of new milk.

Then the June solstice falls.
The rose knows how long it's been summer: a few weeks,
a whole lifetime. Its scent is the whispered word by now
for confusion, for misery, for love. It leans back
against its stem like a spoiled daughter
anxious to please only the boy who wouldn't dream
of touching her. Slowly the street quiets.

It is barely light. Stars fill the sky
several as thorns.

Purple Iris

To cool off summer, we picked up fans
on my grandfather's porch. Winter, as if we could
invent it with our stories,
my brother's breathless lies: icebergs
grinding holes in our meager boats. He said
it froze us, solid.
Penguins looked on, without sympathy
or amazement. We agreed: frozen so, we'd be
ice. We could see
right through each other.

I know that part's true. For now when we argue
I can sit here opposite you in the kitchen
and see right through your ice
to the yard, its shimmer of maple, the lingering
lunging crab apple, past that
to the violet bed, its web of heart-shaped leaves
flickering like a pool. Then one dark iris
probably there by accident, high as radar
on its filament stem. I look
through you and see it
a rinse of light, a perennial startle
of invention and courtesy, and I forget
we are angry, forget we have done this
damage to ourselves.

Pansy

So the pansy, poor annual, never knew
the Shaker woman
who once lived in this house
disapproving the lines
of every locally made chair.

So the pansy never overheard
each century's latest
ruse and panic: just newspaper now
wedging up the far bookcase.

So the pansy's never rattled at our saying
"the sixties" like my old neighbor years ago
in Amherst, Massachusetts
thinking *eighteen* sixty, her father's cloudy reference
to going off somewhere, coming back
half deaf.

All this confuses the lily, perplexes lupine
in their perennial obsessions:
history, elegance, the education of the young.

Memory, my heart says. And on a day like this.

Maybe the pansy fears nothing at all.
I walk past
the high white roses shedding their petals
routinely, like old shop receipts.
Nothing at all. The thought
lies at hand, cool and dark as a mint.

The pansy looks up at me, a white one,
a run of yellow ink within.

I can only do what a mother could,
sitting down before it, speaking to it
sensibly, like an idiot.

Bleeding Heart

Halfway through the ruined afternoon, the girl
decides to cry all the way through supper.
But why this plant along the hedge
weeps at all, how
its runway of ash and tears
breaks off neatly below
the heart, like a pruned twig,
is habit too near
our brain's cool photography. So I passed
the bleeding heart today, one left
on my neighbor's high full bush.
It hung there
like a locket. What I didn't see
till now, till coming home near dark
is how through this keyhole
a summer parlor shifts and creaks in wind,
the lost piano,
the little wooden stool
turning on its strange uncertain stem.

Hollyhocks

Oh, all right, she probably said, you
can take my picture. And your grandmother wedged
herself, like some minor jewel
nearly buried in this ring
of glittering irate hollyhocks.

Years later, you are showing me this picture.
It is trees
we are under. We watch my son
peripherally, dappled by the yard. He pretends
carpenter and doctor, hammering
then healing mute stones. Now a musician
offering his tune as tithe.

Look at this, you tell me.
Behind her, it's Illinois, flat
as patience, conclusive
as toothache. The view, you say, straight,
20 miles to the river.

I see how reverently
you touch the photo, and I watch
the old woman watching us, peering
like someone who endures
only for love
such nonsense. The spikes are giants.
I turn the picture over. In pencil,
not good, it warns. Not good.

Monkshood

They have their vows: emptiness and clarity
and disbelief. In all their immigration
greed is a country
they never enter. Ancient as chant
in single lines they hunch
their small blue heads
above the garden too rash with yellow
anthemis. Monkshood never equates envy

with desire. They envy nothing, not
the sultry peony too rich
for its own stalk, bent down with the lurid
possibility of a Chinese screen luminous
with wings. Enough, they say,
cut back to shroud.
Then it's camera quiet. Shady. Deep now
with other lifetimes, bees
a sudden narcotic. They glaze the garden.

Delphinium

Near the exquisite vulgarity of the chickens
delphinium casts passion
inward, until it purples
into rich targets. This one is lame, splinted up
with a split rod, quickly
like someone lit a fuse and stepped back.

All day the wind's been low static
and near the house the sound
of men fixing the chain saw. Delphinium
could care. About this, or rain
or the chickens busy complaining, outraged
about everything, and dropping themselves
fitfully into mounds of dust. They'd bury themselves
if they could, eyeing the woods
through their little ball bearings.

The delphinium never angers.
It learns quietly, by rote: the stars
are stars. Better to keep grass down, forestalling
violence. The pine is a brother, sardonic
and plain. Genius deepens, a deep

blue thing, too rapid
to see completely. I am this blue, the delphinium knows
vaguely, I am
poisonous. The delphinium loves
the sound of that: *poisonous,* like the true gift
perpetually offered.

Wine Lily

Bees do not care how delicately
the lily's trance
is inlaid, overrunning the garden
easily, like the deepest color
in a bruise. One looks away, for this
is utterly private.
The bees will have their communion.
They come for miles, their wooden hive
stacked up in the low field dropping straight
into woods. Across that road
the town's violinist
teaches children to sound
like crickets. They'll get better
in a lifetime. The bees have
forty-two days. So sunstruck now, they
can barely figure
the scheme of things: how much honey
by dusk, how much sweet depth
for beauty this obvious. They love their rage
and drop it like a dress
for heaven. This terrible red
lasts for days, the lily basking in air.
How the bees release themselves
and rise across the human surface
exhausted, as if they were skating,
pulled by moonlight, home.

November Garden with Moon

Last twilight, I pulled up withered stalks
tomato and pepper, broccoli, squash
threw them off toward the compost pile.

Dazed murmuring overhead, crackle
of stem, whirl of sudden airborne root. It was
half dark, it was a departing room and I was not

gentle, nor was I thinking about spring, some
vague glad rejuvenation. None of that. I stood
shadow and eater, eyeing one small squash

off the garden's edge, an afterthought of harvest
stranded in the weeds. Carrots too, forgotten all summer,
I coaxed them now into dim light: stubby creatures

alert in their brash color, even intelligent, as though
they would walk a few inches for a joke if
I asked. The moon stepped out—an awful

perfect lens. I stopped, then shredded off
the leafy tops. I stuffed them cold
into a basket. Behind some clouds, they stirred,

the elegant friends: planets, the old gods, death.

III

Angels

The boy empties the library when he leaves it
pushing in his chair, not a crumb of eraser behind
not a splinter of pencil. I bury my head
in the entry for snow, the *Britannica,* volume Sa–St
thinking: what use is memory
thinking: of course he's an angel
thinking: he will not know it for a great long time.

Old cars. Computers. Then girls.
His heart will stop
a thousand afternoons, the light
half perfect in the television pulse
all that inertia, plugged in and blaring,
until everything narrows to the sexual instant.

I know he's an angel
like I know certain clouds
new to the neighborhood whose shapes
startle and shame us with their beauty
moving forward on our lifetimes
with their grand so what.

Then his undershirt, off white
so badly worn, it cries out
like a devoted younger brother. I hear it
clearly from here, deep into this paragraph, grief-winged
and wet and boring: *slush*
its whereabouts uncertain, its ambition
amounting, frankly, to nothing–winter
past the brink into a blotchy cranky child. I keep

reading. He is walking by. For to notice him
is to change him. Angels
know the eyes begin deep within the brain, which
is never human. For centuries, they
have been here, and they call
our thawed life a figure of speech,
onomatopoeia, a fake.

Noon

—after the painting by Doris Lee, 1935

She's new at this, that's clear. In studied collapse
against the haymound, she aches to agree, has
almost agreed to everything he glorifies: summer, a guy taking
  his shirt off,
two bottles drained
and aslant in the basket. She does not blink
though sun is vicious and unconscious, this moment
he discovers body and breast and the
deliberate gesture. She only half smiles. Maybe he's
not a jerk. There's the corny bandana, of course, and his urgent
slow motion as if this were the movies—which is what he
promises perhaps, and the rodeo, and the county fair,
  and god knows.
All morning they moved toward this haymound, a buoy
in waters open and indifferent. Indecent now
to stop them with a human stare, after years

trees behind them, trees gaining in certainty
as certainly lovers lose it. Every interior leaf blackens
to delicious stillness. We'd say not wind, nor whistle, less
than that, say nothing. The birds no doubt
have their own opera overhead
where her whispers do not reach, nor his slow wet sounds.

Nothing is opaque as summer. As if one could say
what percent of birds were bone, and saying it, know
anything at all.

Trucks in Rain

Against the sky's rough milk, hills are only color.
And the tarpaulin is a wayward thing
thrown back by wind: glimpse
of wood cut clean, stacked, now stained black.

All night I heard the trucks in rain
and saw their single driver, the cab's dense metallic
solitude, perched high
a tree house above the double wheels.
Old coffee, cold,
the radio at 2 a.m., voices or guitars
scratching like squirrels
behind drywall. And the driver—bored
to the point of pleasure, until it becomes
like sleep, that movie of sleep
where the sleeper is the hero,
the one it really happens to.

I cast this wooden table there
into his dream, offer
this old white mug: all dazed, uneventful things.
So boredom leaks into the world, bare light
from nowhere. I watch it doze
upon the floor. Out the window
of that truck, this place
already is long ago.

Plain Overalls of Another Century

In other centuries, one saw angels
when into the brain some disaster leaked
its oily rattle, right
through a window. You found an angel there
up on the sill. You brought out toast and eggs, muttered
something to the creature, his overalls
plain and of another century. He looked funny, all
at once: *I bring you news, Rodger McBiddle.* He took
another bite.

Meanwhile, we're content to drive our cars
to the mini-mart. Or not content, indifferent.
Or annoyed, perhaps, at prices insincere and overwrought.
In another century, I'd be at each carrot
carefully in the outdoor market. In yet another, I'd be
     starved
and buried. You smile at that, and the glaring
light telling us we *need* Pepsi
shorts out. Shit, says the pie-faced checkout girl.

In another century, she'd be just as pie-faced, you say.
So we collapse this easily
into our own unbearable music: an acre
of glad-hand accordions doing late Sinatra. I walk past
every corn chip in the place—15 kinds—thinking Freud
was right, discontent is a shriveled racket, hardly
equal to this poverty of angels. O to invent one
walking home across the pitted lot, an angel
yes, leaning casually over the stalled dark taxi, his face
a lit oasis.

A Corner of the
Artist's Room in Paris

—after the painting by Gwen John, 1907

How the mind fills a room
with its spare parts: blurred flowers
in a glass equal
the small pale table, equals its single
drawer, useless, probably stuck
by days of dampness. This is not modesty.
The city beyond is less,
bare indifferent shape. These gauzy curtains
dispel its madness, and light
is early, close to sleep, like the ceiling
here, angling what should be
fierce, quietly
into wall. Only in an attic
does the world resist
its definitions so. Wall is wall
and ceiling both. Think architecture
a perverse or muddled study
equal to the heart
in its confusing necessities. One narrows
like a roof
to see what mist
washes everything here: say, memory
of course, say lovely willfulness
that seizes the wobbly wicker chair
and anchors it against
the shabby bent umbrella.
How the mind fills a room
to keep its secrets secret.

Light

—after Edward Hopper

which is not thought, but the airless stare
furrowing its welcome like the inevitable hot
misery of summer. We step in
and out of it. We watch it flood the porch, slice down
hard, windows onto floors. The cat crosses
flares up in angles. And always
someone doing nothing in it. So far away
is darkness, its busy cool imaginings
                               under stone or brick
or think, darkness for years
under the Federalist house. No mural inside
can draw that splendid inkwell up
although the mural weeps where boats
pretend to anchor, and the harbor narrows
two centuries against the impending mob. Distance,
until a man is a drop of paint, a child
bare gem of color, chipped now
some other shape rages, unimaginable toy.
What I wanted, Hopper wrote, *was to paint
sunlight on the side of a house.*
                         But they sleepwalked
for him, their faces beamed up like ice floes, men
and women stunned by circumstance, vacant
as moons. Here
a man on the side of the bed
wakes to nothing. Here a woman floats, dim sentry
at the great bay window. Was it a fine
viciousness, or kindness
that did this? Even the sea is stilled,
its blue the blue
of an eye that will neither waver nor blink
nor recognize in the light, a source of light.

The Heart, for Weldon Kees

The heart is historical, but nothing extraordinary,
no Beethoven or Columbus,
no Tecumseh or Lao Tzu, simply
time after time the finite breath
chaste, the heart
its own doily.

So we arrive in the gleaming red sedan.
The heart is icon then: the Christmas walnut
emptied and painted gold
hung on the murdered tree, the heart
a diligent accomplice
until the needles drop
and burrow into the carpet, motionless
like terrified reptiles

in a Florida drought. O air-cooled heart!
I hear it. Just try
to rattle its door. Inside
the ex-New Yorker dozes in blue
television light, now a game show, now a man
ecstatic to win the dishwasher
the vacation for two: his heart's desire, says
the shiny sun god announcer.

I back away into the sullen lilacs.
Yes, I'll take you away
from all this, I tell my heart
which remembers everything, being historical
but nothing that matters, being
ordinary, being fitful.

A Chair in Raw Hope

The chair sits all night
where there is never moonlight.
The room a thick darkness,
it is difficult to walk.

The chair is simply a chair.
It is our whole attitude toward breath,
or weather, toward a good porch
that will probably outlive us.
Someone made this chair. Someone painted it
this awful color. Nevertheless, how
sturdy it is, how sure
of its own awkward presence.

I say to the chair—take this poem—hoping
for some certainty, some
insistence on the terrible with the lovely
which is beauty in our lifetime.

I tell the poem: you are no longer human.
I tell it: you are better than that.

The Rug

I want to disappear into this Persian rug,
the stilled pale geraniums
no longer blaring their news, past
summer, more solitary than that: stems
in slow paralysis, borders
like roads into twilight, hem of an old black dress.
I suspect we bought this rug
for this: to lie down and forget
a life, see it senseless as a cube
in space, planetary idiot, trash
released out of the cockpit window
into zero sound or air. So we invent
purpose for this rug. I train my eye,
good dog, which moves toward sleep
with only the vaguest intelligence: *this is*
my spot. They want me here. These are flowers,
flat and unshakable and real – ridiculous parades
of them, fountains or pirouettes poised
out of the 20's like a feathery hat. I say
nothing to them. They know
my fate, and go lifeless for me. I drape
my body among them like a thoughtful,
   stupid wife.

Interior with a Violin

—after the painting by Henri Matisse, 1917

Against the war, the shutter opens only
slightly to let the sea leak in,
its boring livid beauty. An underwater light
in the cool black room, the violin
is half-asleep, a warm-blooded creature, its case
bright blue. The eye lets a hook soften
and depart far down to find
this moment. No one dreams
of playing anything, though perhaps
the room itself
is dreamt by the luminous violin. This
or that. Perhaps. Keep going. The violin is always
imagining something else, then lying back.
How the ceiling turns, then stills, to hold
passion here, vented and distracted
in the hot afternoon. There are rooms
we never leave. We close our eyes
and refuse it all: a name, a life,
until beyond, the world can brag of nothing,
dragging its furious, shrinking box.

The Funny-looking Biscuit

Imagination is a city
apartments rented, never owned. Even so
no one hesitates nailing up pictures, the wall
abruptly wounded
these watercolors, a local antiseptic.

I finally find a window. They give me tea.
My hosts have pressed into my hand
this funny-looking biscuit and the room
quiets like a homeless thing. There there, I say,
the kitchen distant
in its squall of voices. What to do, they fraught
over the difficult omelette: so many
guests to arrive on the brink of invention,
inspiration opening like a strange hotel.

But already I've entered the senseless afternoon: not
a wheel or a dish in my head. O street,
none of your cars
sadder than I am, or older
or more inhabited with such little color. And the guilty
    way
we all have
on the way to Shopko for something, desperate
for something: immensity and boredom, what friends
they are. I am invisible before them and their fates
are crossing over the glaring lot. I am also too dramatic.
But the light, I hear from the kitchen, just something
    to see through.

There, I tell my biscuit, I am happier
than I've ever been,
beauty invented surely as bread is invented on the
    nonchalant yeast,
as places come to be slowly,
a stray body of water growing conscious, its boats

absently longing toward a future, as train tracks
inspire godspeed and prophecy. O Shopko! On your blinding,
    killing
mall, I close my eyes: tea,
a rich pendulum. The kitchen: a clock
that chimes. Voices there quarreling toward a generosity called
    decision
where nothing is decided, only one gives in, then
the other, brick by brick,
so the splendid city.

Wallace Stevens and Charles Ives
Talk Shop in Farmington, Maine

Neither really liked insurance,
tending disasters
like unwanted pets. After all, there is
no heaven. They know that
now. No weather ever like a postcard, no claim
to solitude. Like any other
day of work, not even exhaustion, all's
tedious agreement
unlike crickets, like tableau.

They sink into gossip as neighbors do, all
interest in the rose, delphinium, the small blue
forget-me-nots that pine away to pen points.
They stare down
peas and lettuce, doomed
to not quite remember
some crucial innuendo about C.
in Key West. It's hot. Stevens
considers taking off his coat, but the dead
are more conservative than most. He shakes his head
shocked as Ives—at what?
Ives's mouth is a perfect blur: everything

to say, how horns collide
with killing nerve, how these sounds
resist—almost—any reasonable reason.
Yet truth is
the garden is empty, the July afternoon
a rag. I want to lie here, and let
the world repeat itself in them.
They descend
like humidity, distantly
like shifting trucks.

A Summer Shower

—after the painting by Edith Hallyer, 1883

In that century's slow fuse, here is clean cool burn,
careful, a man pouring lemonade only for himself,
remote, a stopped tennis ball. So the game
is strangled by rain. Now they placidly
bore each other under the rich wood beams, still—some
of them—holding their rackets
like picked ferns. It might be all afternoon.
Light pools languidly
over the patterned floor, the world outside
as it finally is, simply absent, details
war and death, fogged as memory. They have no names

these five, but wealth and leisure
and years ago. Dreams divide perhaps for the woman
leaning blankly against the mahogany wall. Over her, a man
angles himself casually as if she might be pulled up
like some fish, gleaming into dull air. What

remains to be said outright is the woman
at the window, the one too big
under the massive black umbrella. So what
if it's raining, she says
with her superb indifference. I like her. How she
chats anyway with someone inside whose posture
is too good to be believed. And no, she will never
never come in. Thank you very much. Nor will we.

The Window

The man has finally hanged himself and rejoiced
sitting down on the bed afterward
saying kindly: little bed, you're still here.
So the philosophers are wrong, he thinks,
everything's here. I am just as I was.
He takes off his glasses to clean them. Outside
a woman is selling fish. Dead
or alive, he shrugs, she'll always
be a fishwife. He shudders at the stench,
those fish flashing up
their sour nobility.
                        In his long johns, he is frailer
more beautiful than before, both the man
on the bed, and the man
hanging near the window, blue
on such a day. He recalls falling
into the soft looped rope
and something thickens, a kind of web
around his heart
for passing afternoons. Good god, sadness,
as if this were the opera, he alone
on stage noticing
the unspeakable designs.
Everything's here, just as it was.
And the man on the bed rises
to the window, perhaps
to acknowledge something
over the fishwife, over her
rotting luminous cart, but no, not
to reconsider.

Binoculars in Dark Flower

The shiny hard-shelled cars
how like ordinary insects they are
from this distance
as we pass the binoculars
patiently, back and forth.
You tell me the world's likely to end.
I know it is possible
as the farmer enters his cycle of madness
politely, siphoning his topsoil
down to the feverish quick, as air
twists in acid dampness, in visible fume
forever our secret unbearable accomplishment
is ruin, and because we
rage with reason: no less pain.
I put my hunger here, filling up
with pure cloud and call it not escape
or reverence for greed and filth of soul
that lengthens on this hill.
I tell you, locked in the tiny glass,
I've been watching a car
for a full two miles: the life walk
of a sand beetle,
the life flight of a million-eyed fly.
Is that all you can say? You, urgent,
pressing the dark flower between us.

Over the Twilight Street

Fall. And the boys are cold, without jackets
the football their milkweed pod
bursting over the twilight street. They jump
and release themselves, crying
like birds. Hours from the morning fog
the air is chilled good water
taken from a stream
with a cupped hand. They can barely keep themselves
inside their bodies, vivid as light
through leaves, though now the leaves
have their own lifetime to consider
pressing back
into trance: a red brilliance
which listens for no one, an iridescence
too complete to translate. I bike by them
the football spinning above me,
a blurred planet. Boys who will be men,
boys who will be taken by surprise
by failure. Again and again the leaves
enact their beauty.

Thanksgiving

6 a.m. Every ancestor sleeps in our moving bodies,
mine, yours, all of us descendants, some coming
hundreds of miles to ease into this tintype. Snow
gathered all night like a grief-struck congregation.

Now someone is up. I hear
a piano in the house below me, soft, like a sheet
falling over furniture. Ancestors hold the wall down there
in portrait, in photograph, against invasion.
They do not smile, brave folk, pre-electricity,
pre–water lines and sewer pipes. A dog
carries on outside where dark
is still a freezing thing, there, where my son and I planted
    bulbs,
laid them gently into their cold grave socks, singing
hyacinth, tulip, narcissus, crocus. They're dumb
as bits of coal
and descending inward. *Descendant.* This trap door

we drop down every day, waking, say,
to no apparent history
but a simple room: edge of window, a shirt
flung over a high-backed chair, the absent, usual coming
of winter light.

The Monstrous House

Old mysteries tumble from the heart
that hidden room of knives
which is defense only
not to be mistook. I mistook the house
for a rosy bed
the road for that gallop
through the child who knows one black wish
as the forest knows the hill, saying, don't rush me, put
    me down.
I knew so many things
which are not: the needle which leaves its eye
upon the porch. Brother to those things
as well— Brother Wisdom
trembling the green nightshade, Brother American Streets
oak and poisoned elm, Brother Sure For A Moment
That The Moment Comes. A bird dives
toward this window where I write
then reconsiders, veering off. Brother Sandtrap,
Brother Solitude. We wait for something
and mistake ourselves
scaling the roof
of the monstrous house
which is, of course, not monstrous
nor even a house.

About the Author

Marianne Boruch is the author of *View from the Gazebo* (Wesleyan 1985). She won a Pushcart Prize in 1988, the Cecil Hemley award of the Poetry Society of America in 1986, a National Endowment for the Arts fellowship in 1984, and she received grants from the Wisconsin Arts Board in 1982 and 1983. She is an associate professor of English and director of the graduate program in creative writing at Purdue University.

Boruch was graduated from the University of Illinois-Urbana (B.S. 1972) and the University of Massachusetts-Amherst (M.F.A. 1979). She has taught at the University of Maine-Farmington, the University of Wisconsin, and Tunghai University in Taichung, Taiwan. Her home is in West Lafayette, Indiana.

About the Book

Descendant was composed on the Compugraphic MCS 100 electronic digital typesetting system in Galliard, a contemporary rendering of a classic typeface prepared for Mergenthaler in 1978 by the British type designer Matthew Carter. The book was composed by Lithocraft, Grundy Center, Iowa, and designed and produced by Kachergis Book Design, Pittsboro, North Carolina.

WESLEYAN UNIVERSITY PRESS, 1989